Craven – Pamlico – Carteret
Regional Library

Nature's Children

TROPICAL FISH

by Robert Hirschfeld

Grolier Educational

FACTS IN BRIEF

Classification of tropical fish

Class:	*Osteichthyes*
Order:	*Atheriniformes* (bony fishes)
Family:	*Poecilliada*
Genus/Species:	*Poecillia reticulata* (guppies)

Order:	*Cypriniformes*
Family:	*Cyprinidae* (carp)
Genus/Species:	*Brochydanio rerio* (zebra danios); *Rasbora maculuta* (dwarf rasbora)

Order:	*Gasterosteiformes*
Family:	*Syngnathidae*
Genus:	*Hippocampus* (sea horse)

Order:	*Perciformes*
Family:	*Scataphagidae*
Genus/Species:	*Scatophagus argus* (scats)

World distribution. Originally native to Southeast Asia, Africa, Central and South America. In the U.S. raised commercially in Florida.

Habitat. Home aquariums.

Distinctive physical characteristics. Generally 1 to 4 inches (2.5 to 10 centimeters) long; wide range of colors.

Habits. Most require warm water temperatures; some are live bearers, while others lay eggs.

Diet. Some species are omnivorous, feeding on both small crustaceans and small plants; others feed only on plants, while still others feed only on other fish.

Library of Congress Cataloging-in-Publication Data

Hirschfeld, Robert, 1942–
    Tropical fish / Robert Hirschfeld.
        p.   cm. — (Nature's Children)
    Includes Index.
    Summary: Describes the physical characteristics, behavior, natural habitats, and care of various types of tropical fish.
    ISBN 0-7172-9077-8 (hardbound)
    1. Tropical fish—Juvenile literature. [1. Tropical fish.
2. Fishes.]   I. Title.   II. Series.
    SF457.25.H57 1997
    639.34`2—dc21

97-5948
CIP
AC

This library reinforced edition was published in 1997 exclusively by:

 Grolier Educational
Sherman Turnpike, Danbury, Connecticut 06816

Set ISBN 0-7172-7661-9
Tropical Fish ISBN 0-7172-9077-8

c.002

Contents

Brightly colored fish can be as fascinating as they are beautiful.

Many people raise tropical fish for the pure pleasure of it. These strikingly colorful creatures are popular aquarium pets, providing owners with hours of relaxation and entertainment. What's more, they never have to be walked or cuddled. It is no wonder that so many people own tropical fish, including all the doctors and dentists who keep aquariums in their waiting rooms!

Raising tropical fish often grows into a lifelong hobby. As they gain more experience, owners can set up bigger aquariums (fish tanks), keep more delicate and exotic fish, and if they like, even breed them.

A beginner, however, can start simply. It does not take much equipment to set up a first aquarium. But before attempting to do so, the new owner should learn a few facts about fish and their habitats. Doing this will almost guarantee a healthy aquarium.

Fish Facts

Nearly all fish are alike in certain ways. Characteristic features of most fish are gills, fins, and scales. But the size, shape, and color of the fish population vary greatly.

Did you know that fish breathe by drinking water? As the water flows across the gills and is expelled, the oxygen in the water passes into the fish's bloodstream.

Fins are used for swimming. The tail fins push fish forward, while the fins on the belly, sides, and back help fish steer and turn. Fish rise or sink in water by inflating or deflating a swim bladder, like a small balloon, in their abdomens.

Most fish are covered with scales, which are bony plates arranged in overlapping rows. Scales act like armor to protect the fish from injury or attack.

Fish do come in many different shapes. Some are sleek and streamlined, which enables them to move quickly through the water. Others, such as the round-bodied kinds, are much slower. And finally, there are the odd or offbeat-shaped fish that can resemble anything from snakes to horses to stones.

Unusual shapes are just part of the attraction of tropical fish.

Even in a glass tank in a living room tropical fish give a glimpse into a strange and wonderful underwater world.

What Are Tropical Fish?

Tropical fish are found in warm climates—in the waters of Africa, South and Central America, India, or Southeast Asia. Most tropical fish sold in the U.S. today, however, are not captured in their native waters. Instead, they are bred domestically, chiefly in Florida. Still, most tropical fish need a water temperature that is fairly warm, about 75° Fahrenheit (24° Celsius).

Like other fish, tropical fish are divided into live bearers (their young are born alive) and egg layers (their offspring hatch from eggs fertilized in the water). Live bearers, such as the guppy, swordtail, black mollie, and platyfish, are fairly easy to breed. Egg layers, such as the angelfish, fighting fish, neon tetra, and zebra fish, require more specialized care for survival.

Many kinds of freshwater tropical fish, including goldfish, come from lakes, rivers, and ponds. Brackish (salty) water fish can be found in lagoons, deltas, and gulfs, as well as some lakes and rivers. The marine varieties, which come from oceans, are the most difficult to keep alive in aquariums.

Getting Your Feet Wet

There are many, many kinds of tropical fish, each with special needs and habits. Choosing the right kinds and best combinations of fish for a home aquarium takes some knowledge. For example, did you know that some tropical fish, like cories, swim in "schools" and should never be bought individually? (Schools are groups of fish that stay together.) Likewise, some fish, such as guppies, are not choosy about water conditions, while others are quite fussy.

Not all tropical fish get along, so it is important to know which kinds are most likely to live together peacefully. Barbs, for example, are ideal community fish, while some animal-eaters, like long-whiskered catfish, happily eat their tank mates!

It is not unusual for new owners to have problems with first aquariums. Sometimes fish become ill or even die or, in some cases, get eaten by other fish. In time new owners will discover combinations of tropical fish that can live together and stay healthy. Staff people at pet and aquarium stores can help fish owners make the right choices.

*Although some catfish are meat-eaters, others, like
this one, are gentle fish that help keep a tank clean.*

Popular Freshwater Aquarium Fish

Freshwater tropical fish are the most common aquarium fish and are ideal for beginners.

Starting out with three or four kinds of fish from the same scientific family is usually a good idea. Guppies, mollies, swordtails, and platys (all of the family Poeciliidae) are some of the most popular live-bearing varieties. They are all small-sized, hardy, colorful, and fascinating to watch. Many owners start with a combination of these.

Guppies, perhaps the most well-known tropical aquarium fish of all, eat both plants and animals. Mollies, such as the black and sail fin varieties, are good for beginners but require brackish water to flourish. They, too, eat plants and animals, as do swordtails. The swordtail is named for the bottom of the male's tail fin, which looks like a sword. The platy, a stouter version of the swordtail, has no swordlike fin. All of these kinds of fish tend to live well together in an aquarium.

Guppies, like these, are popular among people just starting to keep aquariums.

More Freshwater Fish for Beginners

Some egg-laying varieties of freshwater fish also are popular aquarium fish. Many of these are even good for beginners.

Small barbs, zebra danios, and rasboras are among the favorites of new fish owners. The tiger barb, named for its black stripes, eats plants and animals and is happiest living in groups. Of the slim-bodied danios, the zebra variety is perhaps the best known, with its horizontal black stripes. The most desirable aquarium rasbora is the harlequin fish, which can live up to five years.

Tetras are popular for their graceful movements and liveliness. The neon tetra is bred on a large scale. Cardinal tetras are mostly bright red and blue and are animal-eaters.

Catfish, named for the whiskery growths by their mouths, called barbels, belong to several families. Some varieties are good tank fish because they live on the bottom and eat waste food. A good catfish for beginners is the peppered corydoras.

Freshwater tropical fish come with many different shapes, sizes, and color patterns.

A fierce piranha makes an interesting but not very likable pet!

A Fancy Kettle of Fish

Certain freshwater tropical fish are noteworthy because of their interesting behavior. But due to their large size, aggression, or special needs, they are best left to experienced owners.

The leaf-fish is flat and looks just like a dead leaf! In this camouflaged disguise it waits for its favorite food to come along. Unfortunately, this favorite food usually consists of other fish!

Discus, or pompadour, fish are flat and round, like discs. The blue discus are considered the most beautiful of these fish, but they require absolutely clean water and do not do well with many other kinds of fish.

The long, flowing fins of betas tempt certain other kinds of fish to nibble at them. Male betas, known also as Siamese fighting fish, are very aggressive, though mostly toward other betas. Piranhas, which can grow to over a foot long, are legendary for attacking almost any creature they meet, including other piranhas. But they will show signs of stress when kept as single specimens!

Freshwater Aquarium Equipment

Beginners can easily get advice on aquarium equipment from experienced staff members at a local pet store. There are, however, some basic guidelines.

Many fish show signs of distress in small or overcrowded tanks. A 10-gallon (37.9-liter) tank is the minimum size for even a few fish. A 20-gallon (75.8-liter) tank is a much better investment for owners who want to raise large fish or increase the tank population.

Every tank needs a plastic or glass cover to slow the evaporation of water. The cover also keeps dirt out and the fish in. A heater and thermostat are necessary to prevent sudden drops in water temperature.

An aquarium light (attached to the tank hood) is good for plant growth as well as fish viewing. A fluorescent light is best, since it gives off light without heating the tank water.

A filter strains uneaten food and fish wastes. It ensures a clean, healthy tank environment. To supply more oxygen and get rid of unwanted carbon dioxide, an aerator, or air pump, is also recommended.

Filters, which usually are put toward the back of a tank,
help keep the water pure and clean for aquarium fish.

Choosing Tank Decorations

Most people line the bottom of an aquarium with gravel. Store-bought gravel is more likely to be the right size. Sand is not good in freshwater tanks because it will clog the filter.

Aquatic plants help to beautify an aquarium. They also absorb some of the carbon dioxide that fish exhale while providing shelter at the same time. Potted plants that already have roots are the best buys. Artificial plants are also attractive, but many hobbyists prefer the real things! Plants should be bought from an aquarium store to avoid those that may have parasites or other harmful organisms.

Additional safe decorations, such as lime-free rocks and driftwood, are sold at pet stores. Shells, marble, and coral should not be used, however, because they may contain unwanted minerals.

Owners should keep in mind that whatever goes into an aquarium needs to be well-cleaned from time to time.

Brightly colored gravel and plants can help decorate an aquarium.

Tap Water Preparations

Tap water is usually fine for a freshwater aquarium, but it does need to be tested first. Many communities add the chemical chlorine to the water to help kill harmful bacteria. Unfortunately, chlorine can harm fish's delicate systems. Water with chlorine in it should be left to stand for at least 24 hours to let the chlorine escape. Owners can also buy tablets that counteract chlorine. These are sold at most pet and aquarium stores.

Tank water should be tested to see what minerals are in it. Testing kits are easy to buy and use. If a test shows that the water is very hard (has a lot of dissolved minerals) or soft (has too few minerals), it may be necessary to add chemicals. Pet aquarium stores can supply these chemicals as well as advice on whether they are needed.

Setting Up the Aquarium

The best way to set up an aquarium is to make sure that all the items you need have been purchased and cleaned and are standing ready for use. Then, before anything else is done, the empty tank should be placed on a sturdy table or stand in an area that is away from drafts and cold air.

Next, two to three inches (5 to 7.5 centimeters) of washed gravel can be added to the tank. After that, clean tank ornaments can go in.

When water is added, care should be taken not to disturb the gravel. The best way is to put a bowl on the bottom of the tank. Then pour the water into the bowl, letting it overflow into the tank. The tank should be filled almost to the top.

If any plants (real or plastic) are going into the tank, now is the time. Finally, the heater, filter, thermostat, aerator, and light can be set up and turned on.

If everything is working properly, the tank should be left alone for about 48 hours. This allows for the water to be filtered and heated to the proper temperature.

*Since male betas often will fight with one another,
it is best to put only a single male into a tank.*

Putting Fish into the Tank

Fish from the pet store should never be merely dumped into their new homes. Tropical fish are usually brought home in plastic bags full of water from their old tanks. The plastic bags, in turn, are usually wrapped in something to keep both the fish and the water warm.

When you put fish into a tank, the aquarium light should be off for a while, creating a shadowy, more private environment. The plastic bag or bags should float on the surface of the tank for fifteen minutes or so. This gives the water in the bags time to match the temperature of the water in the tank.

Next, some of the water in the bags can be replaced with water from the new tank and allowed to sit for about one half hour. When doing this, a fish net should be used to avoid pouring out the fish along with the water. After that the bags can be opened, allowing the fish to swim into their new tank. Once they are safely inside, the tank cover can be put back in place.

Zebra fish, like these, dart rapidly from one corner of a tank to another.

Healthy Feedings

All fish will eat as long as they can, even if it kills them—and it often does! The time-honored rule is to feed fish twice a day but only as much as they can eat within five minutes. No matter how hungry they look, fish should not be overfed.

There are many different kinds of prepared flake foods, most of which are designed for certain kinds of fish. Some are for all tropical fish, some for plant-eaters, some for animal-eaters, and so on. Goldfish food should not be given to tropical fish (and vice versa). And dry food should not be dumped in all at once.

Live food, such as tiny shrimp and worms, is sold at pet stores and adds variety to a meat-eater's diet. Plant-eaters can gnaw on lettuce leaves stuck into the gravel. The lettuce should be removed each night since it rots quickly.

Freeze-dried foods are also acceptable, but they tend to be more expensive. Many, like shrimp krill, however, can be given as treats rather than as the fish's basic, everyday food.

Daily Aquarium Care

Certain tasks must be done each day to keep an aquarium running properly. Other chores need to be done less often.

It is important to check that the water temperature is neither too warm nor too cool. The filter and aerator, too, should also be examined to see that they are working properly. And the tank always needs to be checked for leaks. All of this should be done on a daily basis.

The fish, too, should be examined to see that they all appear healthy. If a fish dies, it should be taken out of the tank right away. If any fish start to behave oddly, it is generally a sign that something is wrong. For example, when a fish is not swimming upright, or if a normally active fish suddenly begins to hide behind plants or stays at the bottom of the tank, it is wise to consult a pet aquarium expert or a vet.

Other Caretaking Chores

Certain other tasks must be done to care for the tank. The aquarium plants must be cared for each week. Brown leaves (leaves that have died) should be trimmed and thrown away. Uprooted plants need to be replaced.

The filter should be checked weekly and, if necessary, cleaned. Another weekly job is to scrape the walls to remove the tiny plants called algae that grow on the glass. Pet stores carry special tools that make the job quick and easy.

Every few weeks about a quarter of the water in a tank should be thrown out and replaced. The replacement water should be of the same type and quality as the original water in the tank.

Once each month all the decorations should receive a thorough cleaning. Also, rough up the surface gravel just enough to clean it. Every few months the carbon element in the filter should be replaced and about one third of the gravel should be removed and washed.

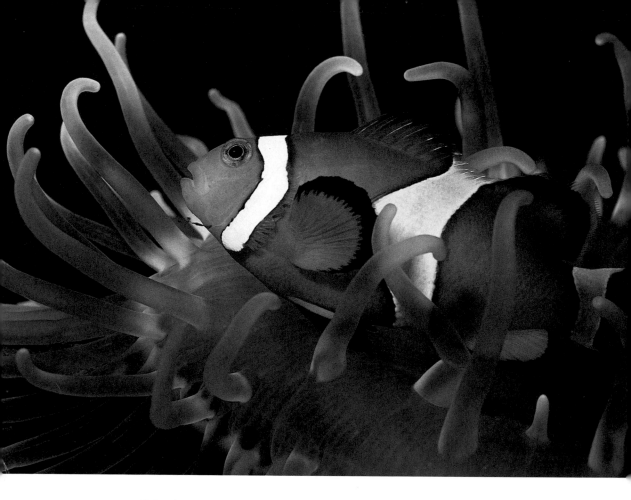

Marine (saltwater) fish often are even more colorful and glamorous than their freshwater relatives!

Saltwater Tropical Fish

In general, saltwater fish are more difficult to raise than freshwater fish. But recent advances in artificial seawater and filters have made it possible to keep these fish more successfully. But it is still important to begin with fish that are less difficult to maintain.

Angelfish are popular aquarium fish because they are both colorful and fairly easy to keep. But owners should know that if there is more than one male in a tank, they are apt to fight.

Clownfish are another good fish for beginners. But clownfish always need to have a partner in the tank with them—an animal called a sea anemone. The clownfish stays near the anemone's tentacles, which have poisonous stingers to keep enemies away. Somehow, though, the clownfish is immune to the sea anemone's poison.

Gobies, like the lemon goby and the blue-banded goby, also are hardy and easy to keep. Slender, colorful wrasses are another good choice, as are brightly decorated banner fish.

Saltwater Aquariums

Although fresh- and saltwater aquariums share many characteristics, there are several important differences between them.

To begin with, seawater rusts metal. Because of this most marine aquariums are all glass, with no metal parts. In addition, marine fish often are bigger than freshwater fish, which means that they need bigger tanks, usually from 25 to 50 gallons (94.8 to 189.6 liters).

These big tanks need more powerful filters and aerators. And because saltwater tropical fish need especially warm water, heaters and thermostats should be set at temperatures of 70°-85° Fahrenheit (21°-29° Celsius). Hydrometers are also needed to check for proper amounts of minerals in the water.

Marine tanks also need the correct water. (Mixing table salt and tap water does not make a marine habitat.) Real seawater can be used as long as it has been strained through cloth. But aquarium stores also sell special mineral mixtures that can be added to tap water.

Beyond this marine tank bottoms are usually lined with sand, not gravel, and they are often decorated with natural or plastic coral.

A yellow sailfish makes a dramatic addition to any saltwater tank.

Odd Sea Creatures

One advantage of a saltwater aquarium is that it allows owners to glimpse some of the unusual creatures that inhabit our seas. Some of these act as strange as they look. Others are quite dangerous. But all are fascinating to watch.

The sea horse, for example, is really a fish, although its head resembles a horse's head. It eats only live food and should be kept in its own tank. Strangely, after the female lays its eggs, the male swallows them! He does not really eat them, though. He just keeps them in a special pouch in his mouth until the babies have hatched.

Pipefish are very long and thin, like snakes. They too eat only live food and probably should not be kept with other kinds of fish.

Some tropical saltwater fish are dangerous even to handle. The lionfish is beautiful to look at, but it can give a very painful sting. Scorpion fish are even more poisonous, and only very experienced growers should ever try to keep them.

The sea horse is one of the sea's—and nature's—oddities.

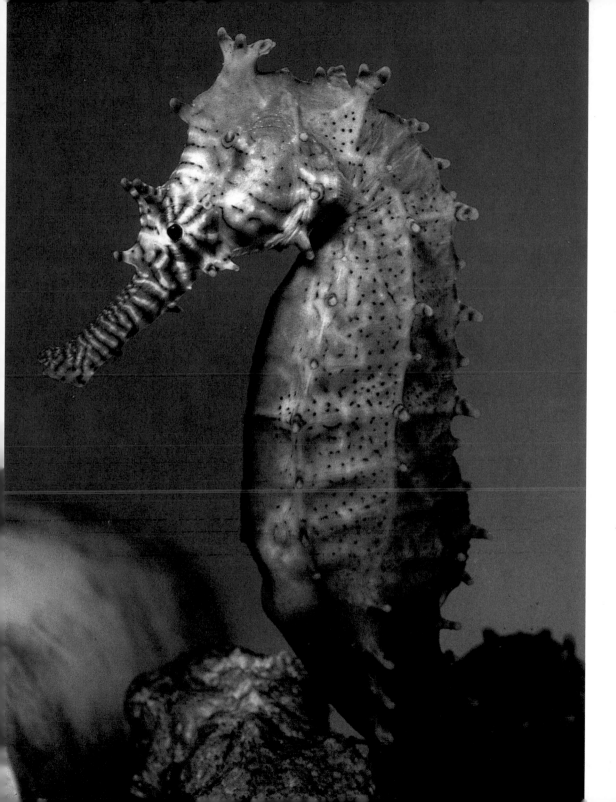

Foods for Saltwater Fish

A variety of foods are especially designed for marine fish. But the basic food is brine shrimp, which are available live or in frozen and freeze-dried forms.

Freeze-dried foods can be fed to all fish, including saltwater tropical fish. But they should be alternated with other foods for a more balanced diet. Flake food is a carefully created food that is specially designed to not pollute the water. Freshly collected natural foods from the ocean should be avoided because they could carry diseases.

The fish should be given several feedings a day of mixed foods. Each feeding should last five to ten minutes depending on the number of fish in the tank. Some kinds of fish may need special feeding times. Some varieties, for instance, feed only in the daytime; others feed only at night. New owners should consult an aquarium store expert or books on marine fish for more information.

A rainbow wrasse—shown here with a cleaner fish—is a good choice for someone just beginning with saltwater fish.

Breeding Tropical Fish

It is not easy to breed tropical fish, either fresh- or saltwater, so the task often is left to experts. But owners brave enough to try will need extra equipment and additional amounts of live food. They also must be willing to spend time and effort caring for the fish and the offspring. Even then breeding may not always turn out as planned.

To begin with, an owner needs to know how a particular species of fish breeds. For instance, live bearers are easier to breed than egg layers. But both types require separate breeding tanks to meet certain conditions that are not provided by the community tank. These breeding tanks often need higher water temperatures and more frequent water changes than regular tanks. And for egg layers tank filters must be shut off so as not to disturb the eggs.

It also is a good idea to know in advance where any new fish will be kept. Unless an aquarium is especially large, adding young fish will crowd the tank. And unless eggs or offspring are carefully tended, it is likely that most or all of them will become food for another fish.

Can you guess why these fish are nicknamed
"kissing fish"?

Breeding Live Bearers

Instead of laying eggs, live bearers give birth to baby fish called fry. After mating, the adult female will produce offspring in groups of about three at a time. Gestation time—the interval between fertilization of the eggs and delivery of the young—is usually four to six weeks. For active breeders like guppies the groups will keep coming at monthly intervals, up to around a hundred fry!

About a week before delivery the pregnant female (who appears to look swollen) should be put in a breeding trap inside a separate tank. (A breeding trap is a plastic container with narrow slits in it.) The water temperature in the trap should be about 78° to 80° Fahrenheit (25° to 27° Celsius). When they are born, the fry will be small enough to go through the slits, but the mother will not.

Once all the fry are born, the mother can be returned to the regular tank. This gives the youngsters room—and safety—to grow. As the fry grow, so will their appetites. Aquarium stores can provide the special live food they need to grow healthy and strong.

This female swordfish will give birth to live young.

These neon tetras are so brightly colored that they actually seem to glow in the dark!

Breeding Egg Layers

Breeding egg-laying fish can be complicated. Since different egg layers have distinct ways of treating their eggs, it is important to know what to expect in the way of parenting.

Freshwater angelfish and other cichlids, for example, take good care of their own eggs and young. But some fish, like barbs, scatter their eggs and then ignore them. In cases such as this gravel should line the bottom of their breeding tank so that the eggs will be able to sink softly for safekeeping.

Some fish lay eggs in enclosed spaces. A small flower pot on the bottom of the tank or rocks set up to make a cave can serve as safe places for these eggs.

Like other betas, the male Siamese fighting fish builds a nest of mucus-covered bubbles near the surface of the water. Then he encloses each fertilized egg in its own bubble, attaching it to the nest.

Pet stores can provide additional information as well as the food that the newly hatched fry will need in order to grow as they should.

Some members of the glass fish family, like this one, are actually so transparent that you can see right through them!

Brackish Water Fish

Brackish water fish need salt in their water, so they are not compatible with freshwater fish in home aquariums. Some of the most common of these fish are mollies, glass fish, scats, monos, archers, and many species of puffers.

Mollies are live bearers that require vegetable diets. The black, short-finned variety is a popular community fish.

The glass fish family contains some fish that are transparent, so that you actually can see right through them! The *Chanda baculis* is the smallest of these. Chandas are suitable for mixed tanks and do well in soft water.

The red spotted scat or tiger scat lives well in slightly salted water. It stays small for a long time but eventually grows to two feet (61 centimeters).

Puffers have the unique ability to inflate themselves for protection. Their inflated size makes it difficult to be swallowed by enemies. Once the danger is gone, the fish deflate to their original size. These colorful fish are quite hardy and not at all difficult to feed.

Pesky Parasites

Both freshwater and saltwater fish are susceptible to a large range of health problems. Many of these are caused by parasites, bacteria, fungi, or worms. As soon as an owner notices anything at all that is abnormal, an expert should be consulted.

Parasites cause a contagious condition called ick in which white spots appear on a fish's fins or skin. Another condition called velvet may show powdery, yellowish irritations. Both conditions affect freshwater and saltwater fish and should be treated quickly. Medicines and advice are available at most pet and aquarium stores.

Fin or tail rot is a bacterial infection that is treatable with sulfa or penicillin drugs. A white, woolly growth is usually a fungus. If fish look faded or have problems breathing, they may be infested with tiny worms or other organisms. Again, aquarium stores can provide advice and remedies.

Commercial remedies for many diseases are available at most aquarium stores. To avoid medicating fish that are not ill, sick fish should be placed in a "hospital tank."

Words to Know

Aerator   A machine to pump air into a tank, adding oxygen to the water.

Algae   Tiny plants that grow in water.

Aquarium   A tank in which fish are kept.

Barbels   Whisker like feelers.

Brackish water   Slightly salty water.

Fins   Thin, flat extensions of a fish's body, used for moving through and balancing in the water.

Fluke   A fish parasite.

Fry   Baby fish.

Fungus   A group of plants that obtain their nourishment from other plants and animals or from decaying plants and animals.

Gills   The breathing organs of fish.

Habitat   The natural environment in which a plant or animal lives.

Ick   A fish parasite.

Live bearer   A fish that gives birth to live babies instead of laying eggs.

Spawn   To lay eggs.

Swim bladder   A balloonlike, gas-filled sac in a fish's abdomen. Fish inflate it to rise in the water and deflate it to sink.

INDEX

Cover Photo: Wernher Krutein (Photovault)
Photo Credits: Dinodia (Omni-Photo Communications), page 21; Chris Huss (The Wildlife Collection), page 4; Wernher Krutein (Photovault), pages 7, 8, 11, 13, 15, 16, 19, 24, 26, 30, 35, 41, 42, 44; SuperStock, Inc., pages 33, 39; Wildlife Conservation Society, page 37.